Building Blocks for Life

Bible Studies From the Editors of *Decision* Magazine

Compiled and Edited by
Dr. Penelope J. Stokes

World Wide Publications
A Ministry of the Billy Graham Evangelistic Association
1303 Hennepin Ave., Minneapolis, MN 55403

Building Blocks for Life
© 1988 Billy Graham Evangelistic Association.

World Wide Publications is the publishing ministry of the Billy Graham Evangelistic Association.

Scripture quotations, unless otherwise marked, are taken from The Holy Bible, New International Version, copyright © 1973, 1978, 1984, International Bible Society. Used by permission of Zondervan Bible Publishers.

Scripture quotations marked KJV are taken from the King James Version.

Scripture quotations marked NASB are taken by permission from the New American Standard Bible, © 1960, 1962, 1963, 1968, 1971, 1972, 1973, 1975, 1977 The Lockman Foundation, La Habra, California.

Scripture quotations marked GNB are taken by permission from The Good News Bible (Today's English Version), © 1966, 1971, 1976 American Bible Society.

Bible study lessons are taken by permission from *Decision* magazine, March 1984, January 1984, June 1985, December 1984, November 1984, April 1986. Copyright © 1983, 1984, 1985, 1986, the Billy Graham Evangelistic Association.

ISBN 0-89066-127-8

Printed in the United States of America

Contents

Introduction

It has happened! And we are delighted. For several years *Decision* magazine has been publishing a significant Bible study selection in each issue, written by outstanding Bible scholars, with practical application to our lives. The response to these Bible studies has been outstanding. Readers are telling the *Decision* editors, "I like this."

"This has helped me."

"I am growing."

The many such positive reactions over the years made it easy for us to decide, "Let's bring these Bible studies together in book form."

You now hold in your hand *Building Blocks for Life*, one of the first four collections of *Decision* Bible studies.

You will see right away that *Building Blocks for Life* is thoroughly biblical, with ample Scripture references to help you glean God's solid truth.

The studies are also practical. They will help you grow. You will stretch and mature in the faith whether you are enjoying the studies on your own, or with your Bible study class at church, or with a study group in your home.

The questions that go along with each study will help you, too. Ask them of yourself. Ask them of your group. Discuss them with others and you will all benefit.

There are twelve lessons in each book, making these studies ideal for Sunday school curriculum. It is equivalent to a full quarter of study in your church class.

If you like the material in *Building Blocks for Life*—and we think you will—see the back cover for a listing of the other three volumes of *Decision* Bible studies. When you have all four, you will have a complete year's Bible study on a variety of topics and themes, written by some of the keenest minds in the Christian world.

It is rewarding to understand God's Word better. It is exciting to have passages open up with clarity. It is good when, with wonder and awe, we can say to God, "Now I love your Word even more."

Roger C. Palms, Editor
Decision Magazine

Lesson 1
Human Courage

Common Human Courage

"Courage is the first of human qualities because it is the quality which guarantees all others."

— Winston Churchill

We have heard how the Lord dried up the water of the Red Sea for you when you came out of Egypt, and what you did to Sihon and Og, the two kings of the Amorites east of the Jordan, whom you completely destroyed. When we heard of it, our hearts sank and everyone's courage failed because of you, for the Lord your God is God in heaven above and on the earth below. (Joshua 2:10,11)

The word "courage" has no exact equivalent in Hebrew. It is expressed by forms of two verbs meaning to be "strong," "alert," "firm," as in "Asa...took courage. He removed the detestable idols..." (2 Chronicles 15:8); or by the idiomatic use of "heart": "With a large army he [the king of the North] will stir up his strength and courage [literally, "heart"] against the king of the South" (Daniel 11:25).

Hence, "courage" is strength in the face of danger or opposition. It is present in all persons, believers and unbelievers. The Gentiles' "courage failed" (Joshua 2:11) at Jericho; and it was the army of Israel of whom David said, "Let no one lose heart" (1 Samuel 17:32). Everywhere soldiers were challenged, "Take courage" (1 Samuel 4:9, NASB).

The religious basis of courage is seen in these examples. The Philistines captured the ark of God from the defeated army of Israel and took it as a trophy of battle to the temple of their god, Dagon. Joab concluded his challenge, "And may the Lord do what is good in His sight" (1 Chronicles 19:13, NASB). Courage based on false religion is self-destructive in the end, as 1 Samuel 5 shows. The courage of the people of Jericho failed because they saw that they were helpless against the God of Israel.

Courage apart from godliness brings havoc to the people of God. (See 2 Samuel 13:28-30.) Man's natural gifts share his fallen nature. Courage alone has limited value. Only as it flows from faith in God and obedience to the Scriptures can courage be called Christian.

—E. Clark Copeland

For Personal Insight and Group Discussion

1. Is courage a characteristic commonly attributed to Christians? Why or why not?

2. Consider the "heroes of the faith" chronicled in Hebrews 11— Moses, Abraham, Joseph, Rahab, and those "others" listed in vv. 32-40. What was the source of their courage?

3. What was the outcome?

4. What situations do I currently face in my life that demand the kind of courage demonstrated in the Scriptures?

A Soldier's Courage

"Without belittling the courage with which men have died, we should not forget those acts of courage with which men . . . have lived. The courage of life is often a less dramatic spectacle than the courage of a final moment; but it is no less a magnificent mixture of triumph and tragedy. A man does what he must . . . in spite of personal consequences, in spite of obstacles and damages and pressures—and that is the basis of all human morality. "

—John F. Kennedy[1]

Do not let this Book of the Law depart from your mouth; meditate on it day and night, so that you may be careful to do everything written in it. Then you will be prosperous and successful. Have not I commanded you? Be strong and courageous. Do not be terrified; do not be discouraged, for the Lord your God will be with you wherever you go. (Joshua 1:8,9)

Three times Moses charged all Israel and Joshua with the same words: "Be strong and courageous" (Deuteronomy 31:6,7,23). God charged Joshua three times with the same words (Joshua 1:6,7,9). Twice the negative was added, "Do not be afraid or terrified" (Deuteronomy 31:6; cf. Joshua 1:9). God knew how much they needed courage to face the giants in the walled cities in the land promised to them. The command points to the premium that God places on the obedience of faith to his covenant promises and commands.

Courage was needed because Israel was to fight God's battle against the enemies of his kingdom (Deuteronomy 9:1-3). Courage was possible because God himself would go ahead of them to destroy those nations before them; he would never leave them nor forsake them (Deuteronomy 31:3-6). Courage must be guided by the Word of God to achieve success. God was, and is, in covenant with his people to accomplish his purpose for them. Through this union he gives them the privilege and responsibility of being the instruments by which his purpose is achieved. Courage is the manifestation of faith that God will not leave nor forsake his people.

Being "a good soldier of Christ Jesus" requires courageous confrontation of that roaring lion, Satan, and all his "giants" in the world around us. Victory has been promised (2 Timothy 2:3,12).

—E. Clark Copeland

For Personal Insight and Group Discussion

1. When Joshua took over leadership of the nation of Israel after Moses' death, did he have reason to be afraid? Why?

2. Are fear and courage mutually exclusive? Why or why not?

3. What situations do I presently face that might inspire fear? What kinds of fear?

4. How can I draw courage from what I know of the Lord?

Lesson 2
Godly Courage

Courage for Kings

"When John Hus was about to be burned to death, they asked him to give up his teachings. Hus answered, 'What I have taught with my lips, I now seal with my blood.' That is courage."

—George Sweeting[2]

May the Lord give you discretion and understanding when he puts you in command over Israel, so that you may keep the law of the Lord your God. Then you will have success if you are careful to observe the decrees and laws that the Lord gave Moses for Israel. Be strong and courageous. Do not be afraid or discouraged. (1 Chronicles 22:12,13)

These words are David's charge to Solomon, who was to succeed him "on the throne of the Lord" (1 Chronicles 29:23). "Be strong and courageous," David said, "and do the work" (1 Chronicles 28:20). David's charge is much like the exhortation the Lord gave Joshua. But Solomon was not to face giants on the battlefield. What he needed, and sought, was discernment and courage to administer justice (1 Kings 3:9-14). The necessity to be alert to danger and to be decisive and firm in action on the throne would not be less than in leading the invading army.

David told Solomon how to face the subtle, satanic attack of wealth, power, and fame; God gives discretion for obedience to "the decrees and laws that the Lord gave Moses for Israel" (1 Chronicles 22:13). Yet Solomon's record, in spite of all the wisdom God gave him, is not admirable (1 Kings 11:1-13;12:4).

Asa, the third king after him, had to face all the idolatry, immorality, and corruption that Rehoboam and Abijah had added to the later years of Solomon's reign. He made a good start (2 Chronicles 14:2-6). Then a prophet said to him, "The Lord is with you when you are with Him. And if you seek Him, He will let you find Him; but if you forsake Him, He will forsake you. . . . Be strong and do not lose

6

courage, for there is reward for your work." So Asa "took courage and removed the abominable idols." He led Judah and Benjamin in renewing their covenant with the Lord and in making further reforms, so that there was great rejoicing, "for they had sworn with their whole heart and had sought Him earnestly, and He let them find Him" (2 Chronicles 15:2-15).

As kings reigning with Christ, we are commanded to give the same courageous service to our Lord (Revelation 1:6;3:21).

—E. Clark Copeland

For Personal Insight and Group Discussion

1. Second Chronicles 15 shows Asa, the God-fearing king, mustering courage to remove the idols from the land. What idols might need to be removed from my own life?

2. Why might it take courage to remove those idols?

3. Twentieth-century Christians in America are not likely to be slain for their faith. What other kinds of persecution do Christians face that require courage from the Lord?

The Courage of the King

"The Bible is crowded with assurances of God's help and comfort in every kind of trouble which might cause fears to arise in the human heart. Today the Christian can come to the Scriptures with full assurance that God is going to deliver the person who puts his trust and confidence in God. Christians can look into the future with promise, hope, and joy, and without fear, discouragement, or despondency."

—*Billy Graham*[3]

Let us fix our eyes on Jesus, the author and perfecter of our faith, who for the joy set before him endured the cross, scorning its shame, and sat down at the right hand of the throne of God. Consider him who endured such opposition from sinful men, so that you will not grow weary and lose heart. (Hebrews 12:2,3)

Our model for courage is Jesus. Fixing our eyes on Jesus, we are to "run with perseverance the race marked out for us" (Hebrews 12:1). The Lord himself has marked out the course we must run— approaching God boldly in prayer, courageously seeking "to be pleasing to Him," fearlessly speaking the Word of God, standing strong "against the devil's schemes," justly and courageously pointing out sin in the church, and supporting courageous discipline. The cowardly and unbelieving will have their place in the fiery lake that is the second death (Hebrews 4:16; 2 Corinthians 5:9,NASB; Ephesians 6:11,19,20; Philippians 1:14; Micah 3:8; Ezra 10:4; Revelation 21:8).

Christian courage is not stoic determination to endure to death. We are called to imitate Christ (1 Corinthians 11:1). But Jesus is more than a model. He is "the leader and perfecter of our faith." He gives us courage through waiting on the Lord for renewed strength, and he promises success in this present life through obedience and victory over the last enemy, death, in the new heaven and the new earth. This victory is for those who persevere in overcoming (Hebrews 12:2; Psalm 27:14; Joshua 1:8; 1 Corinthians 15:54-57; Revelation 21:1,4;3:12,21).

—E. Clark Copeland

For Personal Insight and Group Discussion

1. We are called to imitate Christ. List several situations in which Jesus demonstrated courage.

    a)

    b)

    c)

    d)

    e)

2. How can I imitate each of these demonstrations of courage in specific situations in my life?

    a)

    b)

    c)

    d)

    e)

Lesson 3
Confidence—The Source

Misplaced Confidence

"When you have no helpers, see all your helpers in God. When you have many helpers, see God in all your helpers. When you have nothing but God, see all in God; when you have everything, see God in everything. Under all conditions, stay thy heart only on the Lord."

—*Charles Haddon Spurgeon*

Do not trust in princes, in mortal man, in whom there is no salvation. (Psalm 146:3,NASB)

The biblical message concerning confidence declares on the one hand that confidence is to be placed in God alone. Confidence placed in anyone else or in anything else is a vain act which will lead eventually to judgment.

The most basic form of confidence directed away from God, is self-confidence. To achieve such a position people often place their confidence in some activity or resource which gives them a strategic advantage. They will trust in deception or oppressive violence. They will place confidence in the wealth they have accumulated. If they are religious, they may even choose to trust their own righteousness or ritualistic worship practices to guarantee their security. And foolishly they will construct idols made with their own hands and claim that in them they find their confidence.

Without exception, all such confidence is false confidence and brings with it judgment. For the self-confident and those who secure their positions by deception and violence, judgment will certainly come, an incalculable destruction. The confident rich will find that their riches alone cannot sustain them. Those who trust in others may be disappointed by betrayal. And the maker of inanimate idols suffers a humiliating punishment. "Those who make them will become like them, Everyone who trusts in them" (Psalm 115:8,NASB).

Confidence placed in anything or anyone other than the Lord is vain and can lead only to shame and punishment.

—William J. Larkin, Jr.

For Personal Insight and Group Discussion

1. Why does confidence placed in anyone other than God lead to disaster?

2. Are there people I have tended to trust in rather than trusting in God? Why?

3. Have those people ever let me down? What was my response?

4. What are some situations in which I have trusted in myself? What was the result?

5. What kinds of idolatry are common in the world today? In my life?

Confidence in God Alone

"We trust as we love, and where we love. If we love Christ much, surely we shall trust Him much."

—*Thomas Benton Brooks*[4]

For Thou art my hope; O Lord God, Thou art my confidence from my youth. (Psalm 71:5,NASB)

The psalmist calls us to place our confidence in God alone as the basis for our security and sense of well-being: "Trust in the Lord with all your heart, And do not lean on your own understanding" (Proverbs 3:5,NASB). More than just trusting in him to guide, we must depend on him alone to order and control life's circumstances. We declare, "But as for me, I trust in Thee, O Lord, I say, 'Thou art my God.' My times are in Thy hand" (Psalm 31:14,15,NASB).

God is worthy of our wholehearted confidence not only because he is the Creator and Sustainer, but because he is a faithful Savior who maintains loyalty to his covenant to all generations. Based on experience, the psalmist over and over confesses that God has rescued him out of calamity from enemies or the dangers of this life: "The Lord is my strength and my shield; my heart trusted in him, and I am helped" (Psalm 28:7,KJV).

The results of placing such confidence in God may include outward security and well-being: "You will keep in perfect peace him whose mind is steadfast, because he trusts in you. . . . He who trusts in the Lord will prosper" (Isaiah 26:3; Proverbs 28:25).

But when our outward circumstances are not characterized by peace and prosperity, our confidence in the Lord can still hold firm. We have the confidence that nothing can "separate us from the love of God, which is in Christ Jesus" (Romans 8:39,KJV). Whatever the outward circumstances, confidence placed in God alone always brings inner security.

—*William J. Larkin, Jr.*

For Personal Insight and Group Discussion

1. Is it sometimes difficult for me to trust God to meet my needs? Why?

2. Does God always promise outward security? How do I know?

3. Why might God allow difficult times in my life?

4. How have I found God to be trustworthy even in those times?

5. In what specific situations has he demonstrated his trustworthiness to me?

Lesson 4
Confidence—The Results

Confidence Before God

"Trust God where you cannot trace Him. Do not try to penetrate the cloud He brings over you; rather look to the bow that is on it. The mystery is God's; the promise is yours. "

—*John Macduff*[5]

Since therefore, brethren, we have confidence to enter the holy place by the blood of Jesus, by a new and living way which He inaugurated for us through the veil, that is, His flesh, . . . let us draw near. (Hebrews 10:19,20,22,NASB)

The Jewish Christians to whom the writer addressed these encouraging words were facing a strong temptation to defect from faith in Christ alone for salvation and to return to participation in the Jewish ritual practices of temple sacrifice. But to do this was to throw away the only true basis of confidence, Christ's perfect sacrifice for sin.

The writer to the Hebrews uses the word confidence not only to describe that sense of well-being which we know because we have trusted in Christ, but also in an objective sense to describe the essence of our salvation as a restored relationship with God, which gives us continual open access into the Father's very presence, which we lay hold of by faith: "Let us therefore draw near with confidence to the throne of grace, that we may receive mercy and may find grace to help in time of need" (Hebrews 4:16,NASB).

Satanic pressure from false teaching conspires with our sinful disposition to take things into our own hands. The gospel seems too easy and too good to be true: God has done all the work in creating that bold access to the Father, received by repentance and faith. But the Bible reminds us: "Don't cast away your confidence . . . hold firm until the end" (Hebrews 10:35,36). For it alone gives us an access to the Father now, and when Christ comes, a great reward, receiving what was promised.

— *William J. Larkin, Jr.*

For Personal Insight and Group Discussion

1. How is confidence in Christ essential to my understanding and acceptance of salvation?

2. What does it mean to be *confident* in my relationship with God?

3. In what ways have I tried to "save myself" through self-effort?

4. What does *grace* mean? How does God's grace apply not only to my salvation but to my ongoing relationship with Christ?

Confidence in Witness

"This is a sane, wholesome, practical, working faith: first, that it is a man's business to do the will of God; second, that God takes on himself the special care of that man; and third, that therefore that man ought never be afraid of anything."

—George MacDonald

And now, Lord, take note of their threats, and grant that Thy bond-servants may speak Thy word with all confidence. (Acts 4:29,NASB)

The confidence which should characterize the Christian's witness is boldness, frankness. The Christian speaks the truth of the gospel. There is a courageous quality about this witness, especially when it is given before hostile listeners.

Acts 4:29 is part of a prayer offered by the early church after its leaders had gone through such a situation. Peter and John, full of the Holy Spirit, frankly proclaimed that the source of their authority to heal was the risen Jesus Christ. After the warning of the Sanhedrin not to speak any more of Jesus, the disciples responded in confidence, "Whether it is right in the sight of God to give heed to you rather than to God, you be the judge; for we cannot stop speaking what we have seen and heard" (Acts 4:19,20,NASB). Further threats from the Sanhedrin accompanied their release.

When the church heard Peter and John's report, the members immediately prayed and asked for more confidence in the face of this opposition. They did not ask for the removal of the opposition or even for protection. Rather, they asked God to take account of the threats and extend the witness to the gospel. God answered by shaking the place as at Pentecost, filling all with the Holy Spirit so that they "began to speak the word of God with boldness" (Acts 4:31,NASB).

Such confidence was a gift of God, granted in response to

prayer. Indeed, Paul asked the Ephesians to "pray on my behalf, that utterance may be given to me in the opening of my mouth, to make known with boldness the mystery of the gospel, ... that in proclaiming it I may speak boldly, as I ought to speak" (Ephesians 6:19,20,NASB).

—*William J. Larkin, Jr.*

For Personal Insight and Group Discussion

1. Am I ever less than confident in witnessing to others? Why?

2. How can confidence in Christ make me bolder in my witness?

3. What is the purpose of personal witnessing?

4. What part does God's grace play in the salvation of those I witness to? How can this truth give me confidence as I witness?

Lesson 5
Integrity—The Heart

Inside and Outside

"The acid test for Christian character is not one's actions, but his reactions. What he is before he gets himself under control. What he is before he has time to think and organize himself to make the correct impression."

—*Richard C. Halverson*[6]

Blind Pharisee! Clean what is inside the cup first, and then the outside will be clean too! (Matthew 23:26,GNB)

"Integrity" means something like "wholeness," "unimpairedness," "soundness." The person's whole life is to be consistent —that is to say, consistently good. Thus the word "integrity" describes a person whose character is all of the same quality, and it should go without saying that this means that it will all be of good quality.

Integrity is not a peculiarly Christian virtue, unrecognized by the world at large. People in general know that they ought to be consistent in character, even if they do not achieve it. But it is certainly a value on which the Bible lays emphasis. When Samuel chose a new king for Israel, he was guided by God to the house of Jesse at Bethlehem, and there he saw Jesse's fine, strapping sons. "This man . . . is surely the one [the Lord] has chosen," he said when he saw the eldest son (1 Samuel 16:6,GNB). But God spoke to him in his heart and said, "Pay no attention to how tall and handsome he is. I have rejected him, because I do not judge as man judges. Man looks at the outward appearance, but I look at the heart" (v. 7). Thus the choice came down to David, the youngest member of the family.

Jesus made the same point. He was critical of some of the Pharisees because their outward show of devotion to God and their inward attitudes were not in harmony. Outwardly they laid a great stress on being pure, and thought that they could achieve this by ritually washing their bodies. Inwardly, however, they had not succeeded in purifying their hearts from violent and selfish attitudes. They thought that a clean exterior would cover up the filthy interior. Jesus had to remind them that if they purified their hearts, there would be no need for ritual outward washing, because a clean heart should lead to clean hands. Integrity means being pure in the whole of one's life and not merely in part.

—I. Howard Marshall

For Personal Insight and Group Discussion

1. Why is it important for my inner character and outward behavior to be consistent?

2. Are there times when they have not been consistent? Be specific.

3. When people "look on my outward appearance," what might they see (in addition to physical attributes)?

4. When God "looks at my heart," what does he see?

5. What does it mean to have a pure heart? (Matthew 5:8)

Motives and Deeds

They take advantage of widows and rob them of their homes, then make a show of saying long prayers! Their punishment will be all the worse! (Mark 12:40,GNB)

Although God looks on the heart, this does not mean that the outside does not matter. Integrity means not simply that we have pure hearts, but that we have outward lives which correspond to the pure hearts.

The vital question, therefore, is whether our outward actions correspond with our inward motives. Jesus again criticized some of the Pharisees: they said long prayers and thus gained a reputation for being religious people. These hypocrites used their reputation to entice widows to entrust them with the legal care of their property, and then proceeded to abuse their trust by misappropriation of the funds. Their outward piety and their inward desire to indulge their greed did not correspond.

The point is, of course, that our outward actions should express our inward devotion to God. Faith must find expression in corresponding actions. "A good man brings good things out of his treasure of good things" (Matthew 12:35,GNB). The good heart will not be seen unless it produces good results. When people look on the outward appearance, they may look only on some kinds of outward things; they may ignore the outward things that God cares about. They may be concerned about the showy adornments which are eye-catching and which God condemns, and they may ignore the beauty of the "true inner self, the ageless beauty of a gentle and quiet spirit" (1 Peter 3:4,GNB), a beauty which must be seen in actions or else it will not be of any value at all.

Let us not make the mistake of assuming that only the inward matters and the outward doesn't matter; integrity means that the two will be in harmony with each other.

—I. Howard Marshall

For Personal Insight and Group Discussion

1. In what sense do people have a right to judge me by my actions? (See Matthew 12:35.)

2. Which is more important—internal motivation or outward behavior? Why?

3. In what ways do my outward actions fail to correspond with my heart?

4. How can I help bring integrity to my own life and attitudes?

Lesson 6
Integrity—The Life

Words and Actions

My children! Our love should not be just words and talk; it must be true love, which shows itself in action. (1 John 3:18,GNB)

Just as there must be integrity in our inward attitudes and their outward expressions, we must also be sure that there is consistency in all that we do outwardly. In particular, it is essential that our words and our deeds be consistent with each other. John makes it plain that loving people in need is not just a matter of talk. We may often be able to comfort people by the words that we say, and we should not underestimate the tremendous value of the sympathetic word. But words by themselves are ineffectual when the real need of a person is for active love that may need to be expressed in a tangible form by our generosity with our money, our homes, and our time.

In one great deed of love and reconciliation, God took action by sending Jesus to die for us on the cross. Because God so loved that he gave, he can command us to show our love not just by talking but also by giving.

Integrity, then, means that we must have deeds that correspond to our words. James wrote, "Suppose there are brothers or sisters who need clothes and don't have enough to eat. What good is there in your saying to them, 'God bless you! Keep warm and eat well!'—if you don't give them the necessities of life?" (James 2:15,16,GNB). Words without deeds are dead: "This is how it is with faith: if it is alone and has no actions with it, then it is dead" (v. 17).

—*I. Howard Marshall*

For Personal Insight and Group Discussion

1. What experiences in my life have demonstrated that actions are more convincing than words?

2. In what situations have my actions not delivered what my own words promised?

3. Are words a substitute for action? Why or why not?

4. Can action be a substitute for words?

5. How can I become more consistent in my words and deeds?

God and Other People

". . . As we behold the glory of the Lord we are changed into the same image. It is the work of the Holy Spirit. But we are not automatons; we have a will and a responsibility. We are responsible for what we do about our thoughts, acts, and habits. As we consent to obey God in all three, He works in us to will and do. "

—*Vance Havner*[9]

If someone says, "I love God," yet hates his brother, he is a liar. For he cannot love God, whom he has not seen, if he does not love his brother, whom he has seen. (1 John 4:20,GNB)

If our words and our deeds must correspond with each other, so also must our attitudes toward God and toward other people. One of the most characteristic sins of Christians is to profess a real love for God while failing to carry that love over to other people. John was conscious of it happening in his church where there was much emphasis on loving God and even talk of loving other people, and yet the members of the congregation did not love one another. It should be obvious that the person who behaves like this is inconsistent and lacking in integrity.

Jesus coupled two great commandments: to love God and to love our neighbors. We cannot listen to God's commandments to love him and to love our neighbors and then fail to respond. Lack of integrity is due to a failure at the inward level of our hearts. We are inconsistent in our attitude toward God himself, saying to him in our prayers that we love him and yet refusing to obey his commands. Our faith lacks integrity; it contains some elements, such as trust in God and belief in his words, but lacks others, such as obedience and commitment.

Integrity may well sound like another name for Christian maturity, and so it is. It signifies a Christian life that is consistent through and through.

How can I ever become a person of integrity? Through human effort, it is doubtless impossible. But God day by day renews our lives and transforms us so that we may become more and more faithful to the image of his Son. He sheds his love in our hearts by the Spirit whom he has given to us, and as we let his love control our entire lives so we shall become what he wants us to be. By his power we can become people of integrity.

—I. Howard Marshall

For Personal Insight and Group Discussion

1. Is it possible (according to 1 John 4:19-21) to love God without loving others? Why?

2. Define love. Is it an emotion or an action?

3. How can I love someone who is unlovable and irritating? What does it mean to choose to love?

4. Have I been unloving toward another person recently? How, and under what circumstances?

5. How can I be more loving toward that person?

Lesson 7
Generosity—From God

The Generosity of God

"God's gifts put man's best dreams to shame. "

—*Elizabeth Barrett Browning*[10]

He who did not spare His own Son, but delivered Him up for us all, how will He not also with Him freely give us all things? (Romans 8:32,NASB)

God himself is the primary example of generosity. In fact, generosity is the greatest token of his love, for when Jesus stated to Nicodemus that "God so loved the world," he set forth that love in terms of God's giving his "only begotten Son" (John 3:16) to the world as a provision for man's salvation.

God gives the very best gifts, although these gifts may not always be just what we think we want. Instead he provides what we need (Philippians 4:19). In the Sermon on the Mount Jesus taught that no father, if his son asks him for a fish, will give him a snake (Matthew 7:10). And it is probably safe to say that no father, if his son asks him for a snake, will give him a snake! James declares the principle this way: "Every good thing bestowed and every perfect gift is from above" (James 1:17,NASB).

To appreciate the generosity of God, we can observe some of the things the Bible says that God gives. God gives wisdom in the midst of trials "liberally" (James 1:5,KJV). He satisfies the "thirsty" soul, and the "hungry" soul he fills with "what is good" (Psalm 107:9). This probably refers to spiritual blessings such as justification, sanctification, and biblical truths. But most comprehensively God has given the "earth . . . to the children of men" (Psalm 115:16); "life and breath and all things" to all (Acts 17:25,NASB); and eternal life to those who believe in Jesus Christ (Romans 6:23).

Our response to God's generosity is an important element in God's principle of grace in his dealings with us. Man tends to be legalistic, and he tries to do good works to achieve the blessings of

God. But in God's principle of grace, his blessings lead us to do good works. Legalism says, "Do this or that in order to gain God's blessing." Grace says, "Since God has so generously blessed you in Christ, do this or that in grateful response."

The Bible says, "Beloved, if God so loved us, we also ought to love one another" (1 John 4:11,NASB). As we understand God's generosity to us, we will extend it to those around us.

—*William H. Baker*

For Personal Insight and Group Discussion

1. What are some evidences of God's generosity toward me?

2. What individuals have I known who have demonstrated real generosity? What kind of generosity? Time? Money? Giving of themselves?

3. Do I consider myself a generous person? Why or why not? What does my check register or my budget book tell me about my generosity?

4. How can I learn to become more generous with my financial resources? With my time? With my abilities? With my self?

Serving God

"It is possible to give without loving, but it is impossible to love without giving."

—*Richard Braunstein[11]*

For whoever wishes to save his life shall lose it, but whoever loses his life for My sake, he is the one who will save it. (Luke 9:24,NASB)

The essence of selfishness is "saving" (preserving) one's life. Jesus deliberately uses unusual, paradoxical language in order to shock his listeners into reality. One's "life" here is what he selfishly clings to as important, the universal trait of unregenerate mankind. The ultimate goal of such a life is eternal loss in the lake of fire.

How then do we "lose" our life for Christ's sake, so that we "save" it? Judging from the context of Luke 9:24, we do this by following Jesus Christ as his disciples, beginning with confessing Jesus as the Christ (Messiah) who died and rose again (Luke 9:20,22).

Following Christ leads to worship and ministry. In the Old Testament the priests worshiped and ministered in the tabernacle, and when Paul uses the words "service of worship" (Romans 12:1,NASB—one word in the Greek) in regard to the believer's consecration of himself, he is using an expression that pertains to the activities of the Old Testament priest. This consecration of life leads, of course, to exercising our spiritual gifts as members of the body of Christ, according to Romans 12:3-8.

"Worship," strictly speaking, is service to God (as we think about him and praise him), while "ministry" is service for God. To be acceptable to God, ministry must be generous. Consecration of our bodies in Romans 12:1 implies generosity, as demonstrated in the following words of Paul: "I long to see you in order that I may impart some spiritual gift to you" (Romans 1:11,NASB). We are called to lay down our lives, to lose ourselves in worship and ministry.

—*William H. Baker*

For Personal Insight and Group Discussion

1. To "lose one's life" commonly means "to die." What kinds of death are inherent in following Jesus?

2. What kind of new life results from such death?

3. How, specifically, can I lay down my life in ministry to the Lord?

4. How can I lay down my life for another?

Lesson 8
Generosity—Towards Others

Sharing With Others

"God has given us two hands—one to receive with and the other to give with. We are not cisterns made for hoarding; we are channels made for sharing."

—*Billy Graham[12]*

Instruct them to do good, to be rich in good works, to be generous and ready to share. (1 Timothy 6:18,NASB)

In Proverbs 2:9 the Hebrew words translated "generous" are literally "an eye for good," a graphic portrayal of the man who looks around himself in kindness and friendliness upon everyone. The word "generous" is equally vivid in the Greek: "free in giving."

In 1 Timothy 6:18 Paul is speaking specifically to the rich, but generosity was one of the outstanding qualities of the early church where "not one of them claimed that anything belonging to him was his own." They sold their property and shared with anyone who had need (Acts 4:32-45,NASB).

The law of Moses commanded the Israelites: "If there is a poor man with you, one of your brothers, in any of your towns in your land which the Lord your God is giving you, you shall not harden your heart, nor close your hand" (Deuteronomy 15:7,NASB). Generosity should characterize God's people throughout all ages of history, for they are the beneficiaries of his gracious covenants.

Generosity is also wise evangelistically. Jesus encouraged his disciples to "make friends for yourselves by means of the mammon of unrighteousness (worldly wealth); that when it fails, they (your friends) may receive you (welcome you) into the eternal dwellings" (Luke 16:9,NASB). Through our tangible expression of the love of Christ people may come to believe the gospel and give thanks to us in heaven someday for our concern.

—*William H. Baker*

For Personal Insight and Group Discussion

1. What does it mean to have "an eye for good"?

2. When I give to others—money, time, self—do I often expect something in return? What kinds of response do I look for?

3. What does God say about giving to those who return the favor? (See Luke 14:12-14.)

4. How does generosity relate to evangelism? In what ways have I seen people drawn to Christ through a Christian's generous heart?

Stewardship

"What I kept, I lost.
What I spent, I had.
What I gave, I have."

—*Persian Proverb*

Honor the Lord from your wealth, And from the first of all your produce. (Proverbs 3:9,NASB)

To "honor" the Lord is to obey him, for he has commanded that we set aside deliberately and with purpose of mind (2 Corinthians 9:7) a portion of our income. From the Old Testament this requirement seems to be at least a tenth, but depending on our circumstances it might be much more in proportion to an individual's prosperity.

Generosity may compel us to give beyond our ability or sacrificially, just as the poor widow gave, whom Jesus commended (Luke 21:3,4).

Though the stewardship of our money should be motivated by God's generosity to us in Christ, who for our sakes became poor (2 Corinthians 8:9), there is often a connection between our giving and our physical prosperity. Paul writes, "He who sows sparingly shall also reap sparingly; and he who sows bountifully shall also reap bountifully" (2 Corinthians 9:6,NASB).

—*William H. Baker*

For Personal Insight and Group Discussion

1. What does good stewardship mean? Is stewardship just an issue of my use of "God's portion" of my finances?

2. In what areas of my life am I a good steward? How do I need to improve?

3. Some Christians teach that when we give to God, we can expect a "hundredfold return" from the Lord—that is, if we give a dollar, we'll receive a hundred back. What is the difference between good stewardship and giving with the ulterior motive of expecting a return from God?

4. What kind of "reaping" might I expect from God when I "sow bountifully"?

Lesson 9
Compassion—God's Love Reaching Down

God Is Compassionate

"Love is an image of God, and not a lifeless image, but the living essence of the divine nature which beams full of goodness."

—*Martin Luther*

The Lord is gracious and righteous; our God is full of compassion. (Psalm 116:5)

"Compassion" is both that deep inner emotion to pity and hurt for another hurting person and that merciful decision of action to help. This is the very nature of God (Psalm 116:5) whose "compassions" toward us are unfailingly fresh daily (Lamentations 3:22,23; Hosea 11:8).

When the helpless cry out in great need, our compassionate God delights to deliver them (Psalm 72:12-14). If we feel unworthy of such compassion, we need only remember that it was on the basis of God's fatherly compassion that he made provision for our sin through his Son, Jesus (Psalm 103:12,13; John 3:16). Psalm 103 describes God's compassion toward frail and helpless sinners, saying he is slow to anger and overflowing in love. Yet his compassion treats us not according to what we deserve in our sin, but according to his loving compassion for our needy condition. Such loving care and mercy caused God to send his only Son, Jesus Christ, to suffer on our behalf that we might be rescued from the agony, guilt, and helplessness of sin and death (2 Corinthians 5:21; John 3:16).

God's daily compassion never ceases toward his rebellious children (Nehemiah 9:16-28). Israel stubbornly refused to listen to God's Word, forgot God's work among them and became idolators, blasphemers, and murderers. Yet God did not forsake them, but continued to guide and instruct them, providing the necessities of life and a promised land.

When we sin, the most loving, caring, and compassionate act of

God is his discipline. It helps us see our error, turn from it, and be restored to a right and joyous way of living (Nehemiah 9:27-31). The basis of all restoration is God's compassion (James 5:11).

—Ralph H. Alexander

For Personal Insight and Group Discussion

1. How does God show compassion to me? In what specific circumstances have I experienced his compassion?

2. Is God's compassion to me based on my own righteousness? How do I know?

3. The children of Israel repeatedly turned their backs on God in rebellion, yet he had compassion on them. In what ways have I been rebellious against God? What was his response?

4. How is God's discipline a demonstration of compassion?

5. What kinds of discipline have I experienced? What kind of restoration came out of that discipline?

The Compassion of Jesus Christ

"We never know how much one loves till we know how much he is willing to endure and suffer for us; and it is the suffering element that measures love. The characters that are great must, of necessity, be characters that shall be willing, patient and strong to endure for others. To hold our nature in the willing service of another, is the divine idea of manhood, of the human character."

—Henry Ward Beecher

When he saw the crowds, he had compassion on them, because they were harassed and helpless, like sheep without a shepherd. (Matthew 9:36)

Since the emotion and the act of compassion have the needy as the object, we observe that Jesus Christ's compassion was always directed toward the distress or misfortune of mankind. He hurt when others hurt.

When Jesus looked upon the masses, he always saw hopeless people, mired in sin's devastating effects, and living as aimlessly and helplessly as sheep without a shepherd (Isaiah 53:6; Matthew 10:6; 1 Peter 2:25). But out of his great compassion Jesus, the great Shepherd of the sheep, gave himself as a sacrificial lamb that we, as lost sheep, might be found and restored to him (John 10; Luke 15:1-7). When Jesus saw people helpless, harassed, and downcast, it caused him great pain. He called upon his disciples to help them by turning them to the Messiah, the only One who could heal them physically, emotionally, and spiritually (Matthew 9:35-38). When the masses, hungry and tired, followed him for three days, he had compassion upon them and miraculously fed them. When the sick came to him, he compassionately healed them (Matthew 15:32-39; Mark 8:1-9; Matthew 20:29-34).

In every situation Jesus not only felt deeply for those who hurt, but he did something about it. His greatest act of compassion, of course, was the giving of himself on the cross so that man's greatest need—deliverance from sin and its consequence of death—might be met (Philippians 2:5-11). That compassionate act was done for all—including you and me!

—Ralph H. Alexander

For Personal Insight and Group Discussion

1. What kind of people did Jesus associate with? What kind of help did he give them?

2. Does Jesus hurt when I hurt? How do I know?

3. In what specific ways has Christ shown compassion by meeting my needs?

Lesson 10
Compassion—Our Love Reaching Out

Compassion for One's Neighbor

"People don't go where the action is, they go where love is."

—Jess Moody[13]

But a certain Samaritan, who was on a journey, came upon him; and when he saw him, he felt compassion. (Luke 10:33,NASB)

The two great commandments embrace compassion (Luke 10:26-37). God's people are enjoined first to love the Lord with their whole being. If we have compassion upon others, it always starts by first loving God with all that we are. Otherwise we are unable to love others. The very act of love and concern for others—compassion— can be demonstrated only when we live in the power of God's Spirit (Galatians 5:13-26).

The commandment to love "your neighbor as yourself" (Luke 10:27,NASB) is illustrated by the Samaritan's compassionate act toward the man robbed on the road to Jericho (Luke 10:29-37). Both the priest and the Levite, seeing one in need, failed to show compassion, though their knowledge of God's way should have constrained them to do so. In contrast, the Samaritan, hated by the Jews, had compassion upon this helpless man. Helping usually involves inconvenience; but the compassionate person does not think of self first. Rather, compassion demands the sacrifice of time, effort, and material possessions. For the Samaritan it meant that he had to become involved personally, not just talk of helping. Genuine compassion always gets involved in meeting the need (James 2:14-17). Likewise, compassion does not "hit and run." The Samaritan "followed through" by checking later to see how the man was progressing (Luke 10:35).

The Samaritan's focus was upon the helpless man, not upon himself. He never questioned whether or not the needy man was deserving. He did not stop to "count the cost." He simply had compassion on one in need. This is being a true "neighbor." Jesus tells us, "Go and do likewise" (Luke 10:37).

—*Ralph H. Alexander*

For Personal Insight and Group Discussion

1. What does it mean to "love your neighbor as yourself"?

2. How would I answer the question, "Who is my neighbor?" What specific "neighbors" do I know who need my compassion?

3. What excuses do I sometimes give for not getting involved with other people's problems?

4. In what ways do I try to "help" while still "keeping my distance" from the hurting?

5. In what specific situations could I get involved with helping meet others' needs?

A Gift From God

"Love is the doorway through which the human soul passes from selfishness to service and from solitude to kinship with all mankind."

—*Anonymous*

Therefore, as God's chosen people, holy and dearly loved, clothe yourselves with compassion, kindness, humility, gentleness and patience. (Colossians 3:12)

Compassion is not among man's natural responses. It is easier to have compassion on those whom we like or for whom we genuinely feel sorry. Compassion is more difficult when someone has something against us, who has hurt us, or is our enemy. Thus Paul exhorts us to clothe ourselves with compassion, even forgiving those who have grievances against us (Colossians 3:12,13).

Jonah struggled to learn this truth in a nationalistic context. When God, out of compassion for a pagan and tyrannical Nineveh, chose Jonah to call the "enemy," Nineveh, to repentance, Jonah rebelled. Jonah reluctantly shared the good news which Nineveh needed to hear in her helpless state. He really did not desire that God spare them. God used the picture lesson of the shade plant—undeserved though appreciated—to teach Jonah through his own needy condition to show God's compassion upon those who did not necessarily deserve it, but who needed it (Jonah 4:1-3).

Jesus taught this same truth in the parable of the lost son (Luke 15:11-32). Having squandered his inheritance through loose living, the son became helpless. Humbly he turned in repentance to his father for restoration as only a hired servant. But his father, not even knowing his son's story, felt compassion when he saw him. He accepted his undeserving son and restored him.

Our response toward strangers and enemies in need expresses

our response to Christ (Matthew 25:31-46). Do we have Christ's compassion for the undeserving? It does not come naturally. We must "put on" compassion with the aid of God's Spirit.

—Ralph H. Alexander

For Personal Insight and Group Discussion

1. What does the parable of the Prodigal Son (Luke 15) demonstrate about compassion and forgiveness? How does the father demonstrate compassion toward his wayward son?

2. Why is compassion for an enemy so difficult? Who are my "enemies"?

3. How can I learn to clothe myself with compassion toward them? Be specific.

Lesson 11
Perseverance—Standing Firm With Christ

The Call to Persevere

"We carry not a magic wand, but the cross. And we must understand what that cross signifies: suffering, persecutions, seeming failures. Not the success of the world—but the ultimate and far greater reward of God's approval. His 'well done, good and faithful servant' depends not on our successes, but on our obedient faithfulness."

—*Charles Colson*[14]

He who stands firm to the end will be saved. (Matthew 10:22)

Jesus warned his disciples of troubles ahead—family discord, unpopularity, persecution. They should not expect to be treated any better than Jesus, their teacher and master. The way of discipleship was beset with difficulty and disappointment, and only those who persevered to the end would enjoy salvation in the kingdom of God. Jesus taught that what mattered was not whether they had once given up everything to follow him, but whether they kept on following him to the very end.

"No one who puts his hand to the plow and looks back is fit for service in the kingdom of God" (Luke 9:62). When crowds of people flocked around Jesus, he turned to them and urged them to count the cost of becoming his disciples (Luke 14:25-33). There could be no discipleship without cross-bearing. The rich young ruler who came to Jesus seeking eternal life sadly recognized that he could not face the cost (Luke 18:18-24). Yet some were swept along on a tide of popular enthusiasm until one day they decided they had had enough, and "from this time many of his disciples turned back and no longer followed him" (John 6:66). The meaning of his coming cross proved a stumbling block to those who failed to endure to the end.

—*David F. Wright*

For Personal Insight and Group Discussion

1. What kinds of persecution might I expect as I stand firm in my faith?

2. Have I ever been tempted to give up my Christian life? Why?

3. The early Christians often faced death for their faith. What is the "cost" of discipleship for me on a daily basis?

4. What does it mean to "take up my cross" and follow Christ?

God's Plan for Our Perseverance

"The notion that we enter the Christian life by an act of acceptance is true, but that is not all the truth. There is much more to it than that. Christianity involves an acceptance and a repudiation, an affirmation and a denial. And this not only at the moment of conversion but continually thereafter day by day in all the battle of life till the great conflict is over and the Christian is home from the wars. "

—A. W. Tozer[15]

You, . . . through faith are shielded by God's power until the coming of the salvation that is ready to be revealed in the last time. (1 Peter 1:4,5)

The perseverance of God's people is part of what God has planned for them. As Paul wrote to the Christians of Philippi, "He who began a good work in you will carry it on to completion until the day of Christ Jesus" (Philippians 1:6). We acknowledge God's gracious power in bringing us to faith in Christ but too often imagine that our endurance depends on our effort alone. But Christ is our Shepherd, not only rescuing us when we were lost but also taking care of us for the rest of life: "I give them eternal life, and they shall never perish; no one can snatch them out of my hand" (John 10:28).

Our final perseverance is an aspect of the gift of salvation: "My Father's will is that everyone who looks to the Son and believes in him shall have eternal life," says Jesus, "and I will raise him up at the last day" (John 6:40). Jesus binds together the beginning of faith and the final resurrection. Paul explains that we who have died with Christ share a life hidden with Christ in God; when Christ, our hidden life, is revealed to all creation, we too will appear with him in glory (Colossians 3:3,4).

The Christian's endurance to the end by the power of God is thus implied in all the great doctrines of salvation. They teach us to view our experience of being a Christian in the context of God's purpose to call out a people whose chief end is "to glorify God and to enjoy him for ever," as the Westminster Shorter Catechism puts it. God's people are chosen for a destiny of eternity, and he is fully able to accomplish what he plans for them. There is nothing surprising in this for those who know that their new life in Christ is all of grace. If God did not spare his very own Son but surrendered him up for us, how can he fail to give us all that we need to persevere to the end?

—*David F. Wright*

For Personal Insight and Group Discussion

1. How secure is my life in Christ? How do I know? (See John 6:40.)

2. Do I often act as if I alone am totally responsible for my Christian life? Why?

3. Who is responsible for making me into the image of Christ? (See Philippians 1:6.) What is my part in the transformation process?

4. How can an assurance of perseverance to the end of my Christian life affect how I live from day to day?

Lesson 12
Perseverance—Standing Firm in Suffering

Persevering Under Trials

"Our suffering is not worth the name of suffering. When I consider my crosses, tribulations, and temptations, I shame myself almost to death, thinking what are they in comparison to the sufferings of my blessed Saviour Christ Jesus."

—*Martin Luther*

Blessed is the man who perseveres under trial, because when he has stood the test, he will receive the crown of life that God has promised to those who love him. (James 1:12)

The place of "the perseverance of the saints" in God's plan does not exempt us from trial and tribulation, but gives us the confidence to carry on through them and despite them—and even to benefit from them! The life of discipleship is not one of unsullied delight, marked only by peace, happiness, and prosperity. It is a cruel deception to lead Christians to expect a trouble-free existence once they have committed themselves wholly to Jesus Christ. What they can and must be assured of is that in the hardest struggle and the bleakest "night of the soul!" they are kept by the power of God.

The challenge to persevere in adversity is a necessary stage in our Christian growth: "Consider it pure joy, my brothers, whenever you face trials of many kinds, because you know that the testing of your faith develops perseverance. Perseverance must finish its work so that you may be mature and complete, not lacking anything" (James 1:2-4). There is no place here for mock heroics—no spiritual bravado or voluntary martyrdom, but rather the sobering and deeply encouraging awareness that the author of our salvation was made perfect through suffering and learned thereby what obedience really meant (Hebrews 5:8). The experience of suffering, if it produces perseverance, far from casting us down into despair, refines our character.

But often perseverance is not a matter of enduring calamities

46

and harassment, but simply of faithful persistence. The calling of the Christian is to continue unstintingly—forgiving others "seventy times seven" (Matthew 18:22,KJV), witnessing to the gospel "in season, out of season" (2 Timothy 4:2,KJV), giving oneself fully to the work of the Lord "while it is day" (John 9:4,KJV), never tiring of unselfish service. Above all, perseverance is tested in prayer. Paul ends his picture of the Christian's armor with a summons to prayer: "Pray in the Spirit on all occasions with all kinds of prayers and requests. With this in mind, be alert and always keep on praying for all the saints" (Ephesians 6:18).

—David F. Wright

For Personal Insight and Group Discussion

1. Often people are misled into accepting an easy Christianity: "Come to Jesus and all your problems will be solved." What is the result of such belief in light of reality?

2. What purpose does difficulty serve in my life? (See James 1:2-4.)

3. How do I usually respond to "trials of many kinds"? What are some other possible responses?

4. How does a knowledge of God's love and faithfulness affect my response to adversity?

God Perseveres for Us and With Us

"No true believer is Christlike at the beginning of his Christian life. Little by little, day by day, we grow into the measure of the stature of the fullness of Christ; it is a lifelong process, and at the end there is still a vast gap that must be bridged by the transforming power of Christ in our glorification together with Him. The true meaning of the phrase, 'If any man have not the Spirit of Christ, he is none of his,' lies rather in the presence of divine life, the germ from which Christlikeness may develop. "

—*Donald Grey Barnhouse*[16]

Let us fix our eyes on Jesus, the author and perfecter of our faith, who for the joy set before him endured the cross, scorning its shame, and sat down at the right hand of the throne of God. (Hebrews 12:2)

Jesus is the great perseverer. The Letter to the Hebrews leads its readers in chapter 11 through faith's hall of fame. The lives of these men and women spoke volumes about what God's people can suffer and achieve "by faith." Amid such a galaxy we too must "run with perseverance the race marked out for us," (Hebrews 12:1) with our eyes fixed on Jesus, who endured—as no one else has endured—the burden of the world's sin on the cross. When we keep before our eyes what he suffered for us, how can we fail to follow in his path of patient endurance, bearing our cross after him? As we fasten our gaze on the Christ who bore our sins all the way to the cross, he "perfects" our faith, for he was made perfect by suffering.

In Gethsemane Jesus most intensely persevered in the Father's will for his life, which required his death. Jesus struggled alone in prayer, overwhelmed by anguish, sweating drops of blood. But he persevered triumphantly for us and for our salvation.

We need to remember that our Father perseveres with us to the very last. His steadfast love is not moody or fitful. He does not fall out of love with us when we turn our back on his will. He is a God of infinite patience who bears with his wayward children. His discipline may be so painful that we may feel as if he has cast us off, but he does not abandon us. We may grow faint and stumble, but God will not grow tired or weary. His faithfulness to us endures forever.

—David F. Wright

For Personal Insight and Group Discussion

1. How does "fixing my eyes on Jesus" help me to endure the weariness that inevitably comes in life's struggles?

2. What kinds of "suffering" do I experience? In what specific ways has Jesus experienced comparable sufferings?

3. When God disciplines me, how can I interpret that as a sign of his unfailing love? (See Hebrews 12:5-11.)

4. Under what circumstances have I been let down by the inconsistency of a friend's love? How can I learn to depend more fully on the consistent, faithful love of God?

Notes

[1] Quoted in George Sweeting, *Great Quotes and Illustrations* (Waco, Texas: Word, 1985), 73.

[2] Ibid.

[3] Ibid.

[4] Quoted in Frank S. Mead, *Encyclopedia of Religious Quotations* (Old Tappan, New Jersey: Fleming H. Revell, 1965), 448.

[5] Ibid., 449.

[6] Richard C. Halverson, *Christian Maturity* (Los Angeles: Cowman, 1956), 78.

[7] Arthur F. Holmes, *Contours of a World View* (Grand Rapids, Michigan: Wm. B. Eerdmans, 1983), 117.

[8] Robert E. Speer, *Seeking the Mind of Christ* (Old Tappan, New Jersey: Fleming H. Revell, 1926), 61.

[9] Vance Havner, *Pleasant Paths* (Old Tappan, New Jersey: Fleming H. Revell, 1945), 74.

[10] Elizabeth Barrett Browning, "Sonnets from the Portuguese," no. 26.

[11] Quoted in Mead, *Religious Quotations,* 159.

[12] Ibid., 160.

[13] Quoted in Sweeting, *Great Quotes,* 175.

[14] Charles Colson, *Who Speaks for God?* (Westchester, Illinois: Crossway, 1985), 33.

[15] A. W. Tozer, *That Incredible Christian* (Camp Hill, Pennsylvania: Christian Publications, 1964), 74.

[16] Donald Grey Barnhouse, *The Cross Through the Open Tomb* (Grand Rapids, Michigan: Eerdmans, 1961), 133.

About the Authors

E. Clark Copeland, Th.D.,
is professor of Old Testament at the Reformed Presbyterian Theological Seminary in Pittsburgh, Pennsylvania, and was for thirteen years a missionary to Cyprus.

William J. Larkin, Jr., Ph.D.,
is professor of New Testament and Greek at Columbia Biblical Seminary and Graduate School of Missions, Columbia, South Carolina.

I. Howard Marshall
is professor of New Testament exegesis at the University of Aberdeen in Scotland. He is the author of several books, including a commentary, *1 and 2 Thessalonians,* and *Biblical Inspiration.*

William H. Baker
is professor of Bible and theology at Moody Bible Institute, Chicago, Illinois, and is the author of the books *On Capital Punishment,* and *Sanctification: Why We Resist God, How to Overcome It.*

Ralph H. Alexander, Th.D.,
is professor of Hebrew Scripture at Western Conservative Baptist Seminary in Portland, Oregon, and the author of numerous articles on biblical themes.

David F. Wright
is senior lecturer in ecclesiastical history and dean of the faculty of divinity at New College, University of Edinburgh, Scotland, and author and editor of several scholarly works.